People of the Plains

Kenya's People
edited by Margaret Sharman

Margaret Sharman

Evans Brothers Limited

Published by Evans Brothers Limited
Montague House, Russell Square
London WC1B 5BX

Evans Brothers (Nigeria Publishers) Limited
PMB 5164, Jericho Road
Ibadan

First published 1979

Illustrated by John Ochieng' and Gay Galsworthy

Photographs by Cynthia Salvadori and Vincent Oliver

Filmset in 11/12 point Baskerville and printed in Great Britain by
BAS Printers Limited, Over Wallop, Hampshire

ISBN 0 237 49894 4   PRA 6438

Contents

Illustrations

Acknowledgements

The author would like to thank John Sirere ole Sailenyi and Dr Paul Spencer for reading the manuscript and making valuable comments and suggestions, and Dr Alan Jacobs for advice on the Maasai homelands before 1800.

Foreword

The Maasai are perhaps the most well-known of all Kenya groups to outsiders, and many travellers of the late nineteenth century told tales of their bravery and courage. The Arab slave-traders feared them and avoided their lands, but they also exaggerated their fierceness to stop other traders from visiting them.

When you read other books on the Maasai you may find that descriptions of their way of life differ in detail from those given here. Different sections of the Maasai have slightly different customs, and I have had to generalize in this short book. In particular I have not mentioned the generation-sets of the Maasai, since this is too difficult a subject to present in a short space.

Many of the older books about the Maasai are difficult to obtain, and one of the best is written in German. However, a recent account has been given by S. S. ole Sankan in his book *The Maasai*, published by the East African Literature Bureau.

Margaret Sharman
British Institute in Eastern Africa

1 Their Homeland

The Maasai people identify themselves as all those who speak the language Ol-maa. There is a wide variety of dialects of this language, and the different branches of Maasai peoples are known by different names, though they are basically all one people. The map on page 3 shows the different Maasai groups in Kenya and Tanzania today. As you will see, the Maasai country cuts right across the border, and occupies much of central Kenya and northern Tanzania, along the path of the great Rift Valley. In the north, the Samburu live in a semi-desert, with camels as well as the traditional cattle of the rest of the Maasai. Their lands are the most waterless, and they have to move often to follow the drying-up grazing grounds. Further south the savannah country grows thorn bushes and scrub-land which is no good for agriculture, but as long as the wells are full, is adequate for grazing cattle, sheep and goats. The Maasai depend on wells, rivers (both permanent and seasonal) and springs; when these dry up they are compelled to move on to wetter country.

So in order to fit in with the lands they occupy, the Maasai have remained a pastoral people, depending for their living on the cattle, sheep and goats they own. They are semi-nomadic—that is, they build houses and cattle-pens, but they do not stay in one place all the time. The question of water makes this impossible.

Before they lived in the south of the country we now call Kenya, the Maasai people probably grazed their cattle around Lake Turkana. Why they moved we do not know, but many generations ago (in about 1700) they moved first into the fertile plains stretching from Mount Elgon to Mount Kenya. They lived in this area for many years, gradually expanding. In the Rift Valley they found a people we call

1

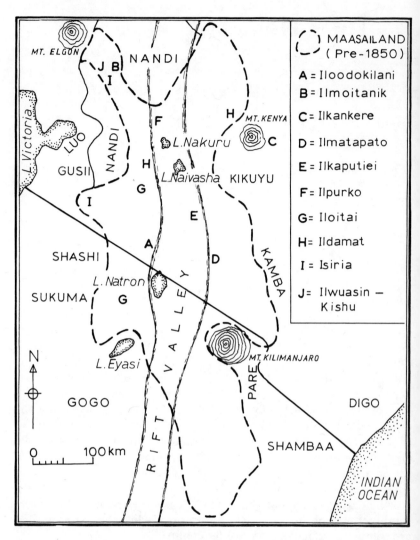

Fig. 1   The Maasai formerly grazed over much more land in Kenya than they do today. In Tanzania the area is much the same as it was 150 years ago, though a great deal of it is now shared with the country's most famous game parks.

the Sirikwa, also cattle-keepers, and the builders of small circular earth shelters for their animals. Before the Maasai arrived these shelters were quite sufficient to keep out thieves or wild animals, but they were not strong enough to withstand the raiding Maasai. The remains of these circles can still be seen today: they are known as 'Sirikwa holes'.

2

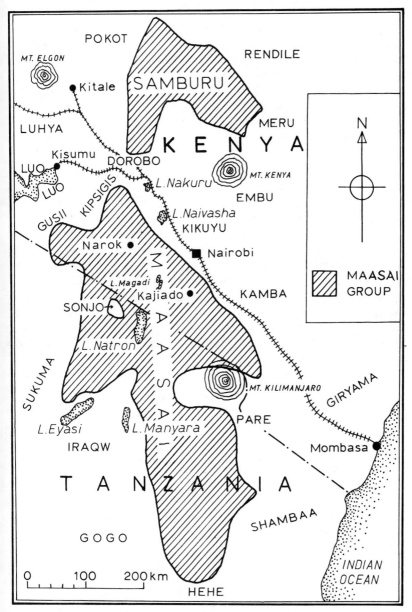

Fig. 2 The Maasai live in both Kenya and Tanzania. The Kenya Maasai occupy an area set aside for them during this century; they were then no longer allowed to occupy their old northern lands.

By 1800 the Maasai had spread far to the south, past Lake Natron, past Kilimanjaro, deep into today's Tanzania. The area they grazed over was far greater then than their lands are today (fig.2). They ruled

3

the interior of East Africa, and they were feared by the neighbouring Bantu tribes. Because of their reputation as warriors the Arab traders avoided their lands, and so this part of Africa was almost free from the slave raids and civil wars that destroyed so many villages and settlements in other areas.

In the south, the Maasai were stopped in their advance by the Hehe and the Gogo, and those Maasai-speakers now living in the south have built permanent villages and planted crops. But the northern Maasai kept their pastoral habits, and can still be seen herding their cattle in the scrub-lands of central Kenya.

But today, as we have seen, their territory is not so huge as it once was. In 1910–11 the Maasai were forced by the colonial government to live in a reserve in southern Kenya (fig. 2). Although the area looks very large, it is only a fraction of the old Maasai grazing grounds, and some of it is unusable. If you look at a map of Kenya's game reserves, you will see that some of the Maasai land has to be shared with wild animals. This has led to a constant battle between the Maasai and the game wardens. For instance, the Maasai are inclined to graze their cattle along fixed trails as they lead them to water, whereas wild animals when they graze, spread out over a wider area. The Maasai cattle are thus more likely to cause soil erosion, which in time leads to a great scarcity of grass and water, and affects the lives of all the human and animal inhabitants of the area.

The Maasai Groups

In Kenya, the Maasai are divided up into sections, as follows:

Administered from Kadjiado: Iloodokilani—Iloitokitok (or Ilkisonko)—Ilkeekonyokie—Ilkankere (or Ildalale Kutuk)—Ilmatapato—Ilkaputiei.

Administered from Narok: Ilpurko—Iloitai—Ildamat—Isiria—Ilwuasin-Kishu—Ilmoitanik.

It is not necessary to remember all these names, but it is interesting to know that there are so many sections of Maasai. They are all quite separate, but they all keep more or less the same customs, and have the same organization.

Clans

The clan system runs right through all the above sections. A Maasai, whether he be of the Ilpurko, or Ilkaputiei, or Iloitai section, can belong also to one of these five clans:

Ilmakesen—Ilaiser—Ilmolelian—Iltarrosero—Ilukumae. Each clan has its own cattle brand (some clans have more than one) and in

4

this manner a man knows the clans to which his friends belong. This is important, because a man may not normally marry a girl who is of the same clan, and so has the same cattle brand as himself.

2 How the Maasai Live

Let us see how a typical Maasai man or woman lives, what their houses are like, what they eat, and how they pass their time.

The House

First, the boys and girls when they are children live with their mother in a house built of mud-and-wattle, in a large enclosure, and their father's other wives and young children live nearby in houses of their own. There is a small house called *orripie* where the father of the family lives. Near them, in the same enclosure, there may be other families, grouped together in a collection of mud-and-wattle houses. All round these houses is a thorn fence for protection.

The houses in the enclosure are arranged in a special fashion. Each family has a doorway (perhaps two) in the thorn fence round the enclosure. The first wife's house is built on the right of the doorway, and here she lives with her young children. If her husband marries a second wife, this wife builds her house on the left of the doorway. A third wife lives on the right, next to the first wife, and so on, the wives living alternately to the right and left of the opening in the thorn fence.

This type of homestead is called *enkang*, and may have twenty or even thirty houses in it, in a circle. The livestock can be penned up in the middle of the enclosure at night time. During the night, and in times of danger, the gateways are filled in with brushwood to make a solid fence. Since one man may own 75 cows, the same number of sheep and goats, and a dozen or so donkeys, the enclosure can become crowded at night.

Nobody is likely to live in the same house all his life, unless he dies young. As we have seen, Maasai homesteads are often moved about, when grazing becomes poor and seasonal rivers dry up. Then the business of house-building starts again.

To build a house the women mark out an oblong, about two by three metres in size. They make small scooped-out holes around this oblong, and put cow-dung into them to soften the soil. These holes are made at about 12 cm intervals, leaving a space for a door, which will later be made of bamboo or other strong poles. They then collect a number of

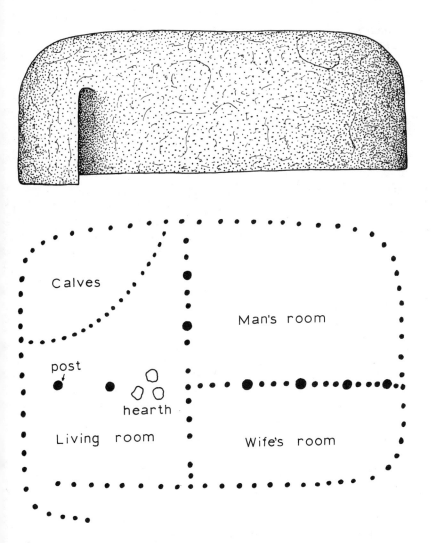

Fig. 3   This is how a Maasai house looks, inside and outside. As it has no windows, it is quite dark inside. There is a small hole in the roof above the fireplace.

long stakes or poles, which they drive into the holes as though they were pounding grain. When the pole is deep enough into the ground they pack it in with earth so that it stands firmly. These poles, which are about one and a half or two metres high, are the beginnings of the walls of the house. The women then collect thin 'whippy' branches, peel the bark off, and tie them to the uprights near the top, at right-angles, so that they are joined together all round. Saplings are pushed between the horizontal ties and the uprights, and fastened together across the top of the hut, making a curved roof. This is the first stage in hut building. Next the women collect a quantity of twigs and small branches, with which they fill in the spaces between the stakes. They then plaster cow-dung all over the wooden structure, adding several layers of the mixture to make the walls and roof thick and smooth. The sun does the rest, for it bakes the dung hard enough to keep out the rain. (If the roof later begins to leak, more cow-dung is added.) A small hole is left in the top of the house, for the cooking fire is built inside, and the smoke must have an escape route. Sometimes other holes are left open to provide more light.

A Maasai house has very little furniture, for people who tend to move about do not acquire many possessions. The cooking pots are there, and a stool or two for sitting on. There is a low bed, made of hides and poles, for the woman, and another for her children. She has to leave room in her house for calves and a wood store, and a small fireplace. As there are no windows in the house, it takes time for eyes used to the sunlight to accustom themselves to the dark interior.

Food and Trading

In the old days, the Maasai lived almost entirely off their cattle, drinking their milk and blood and occasionally eating meat. But even then, these foods were supplemented (except for the warriors) by vegetables and grain, which were obtained from the Bantu nearby, and, particularly (in Kenya), the Kikuyu. The Kikuyu like Maasai hides, milk and butter, and they exchanged them by barter for beans, millet, tobacco, red ochre and sugar cane.

Markets were set up in different places on the boundaries of Kikuyuland, and Maasai women could fairly easily find one of these trading places within walking distance (though sometimes they walked for several days). It was always the older women who took the hides, cows (usually old ones) and milk to the market, and the Kikuyu women looked after their own agricultural produce. Even when the two peoples were at war with one another, the women were allowed to pass between the two sides for trade. The Kikuyu greatly admired the Maasai, copying their weapons, headgear, and customs.

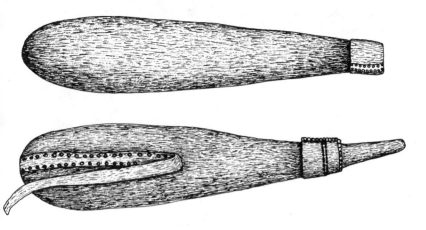

Fig. 4   Gourds used for collecting blood and milk.

As well as this trade with the Kikuyu, the Maasai obtained honey (for making honey-wine) from the forest-dwellers known as the Iltorrobo (Dorobo). Besides being wonderful honey-collectors, the Dorobo were keen hunters and the Maasai obtained from them ivory for ornaments.

Fig. 5   Blood is obtained by shooting a small arrow into the cow's neck.

3   Childhood

The children had plenty of playmates of their own age, and they got used to living near other families from birth. Boys played all kinds of imaginative games together, and girls sometimes had dolls, which their mothers made for them out of clay.* Children learnt the family traditions and customs as soon as they could understand them. Their mothers told them stories, riddles and proverbs, which they then told to each other. As soon as they were old enough they learnt about clans and cattle brands, who was related to whom, and what they might or might not eat. They lived mainly on milk, with occasional meat dishes, and vegetables which their mothers, and their older sisters, obtained by barter from the agricultural Bantu peoples.

At about four years old, both boys and girls had their two lower front teeth removed. This is a custom followed by many African peoples. It is said to be a precaution against tetanus, a disease which makes a person clench his teeth so hard that he is unable to open his mouth. If two of his teeth have been removed, he can be fed through the gap. The disease is caused by a minute organism in the soil, particularly in places where cattle graze.

At the same time holes were pierced in the tops and lobes of their ears, and sharp sticks pushed through the holes to widen them. As time went on they used bigger sticks, then large bone or wooden ear-plugs, so that when the children were grown up their ear-lobes were long enough to hold big ornaments.

---

*Customs and ceremonies are fast changing as the Maasai come into contact with urban conditions. The next sections are written in the past tense, but in many areas of Kenya the Maasai of today still follow these customs.

A boy, as soon as he was about seven years of age, went with his elder brothers or friends to learn how to herd cattle. He learnt about the best places for grazing cattle, how to look after calves and lambs in the bush, and to recognize his own family's cows. His sister stayed at home with her mother and female relations, helping to sweep the house, milk the cows, cook, draw water, scrape and sew skins, and thread necklaces. A child up to the age of fifteen had few rights and privileges, but he enjoyed himself playing games, throwing small spears, jumping, and hunting birds.

Initiation

One day a group of boys arrived at the homestead. They were about fifteen or sixteen years old, and they were recruiting other boys of the same age for the next 'grade'—circumcision and the end of childhood. The young boys went from village to village asking that their case be taken up by the elders. They were given gifts of hyrax skins and honey. When the elders agreed that circumcision should take place, the boys staged an ox-fighting contest, when they had to try to seize the horns of a black ox. At the end of the fight the ox was killed and small rings were made of its hide, which the boys wore for a few days. Now that it was agreed they should be circumcised, the boys had to learn about their new role in life. They learnt from an elder how to behave to women and to elders, how to enter a house, the proper behaviour when eating and drinking, how to raid cattle, and how to fight. They were the candidates for warriorhood.

The elders chose one of the boys to be the leader of the group (he was called *Olaiguanani*), and he often remained their leader until the youths became elders.

The boys then waited quietly at home to be circumcised by an elder who was not usually a true Maasai. The man who performed the operation went from one enclosure to another, and it might take him two or three months to get all round. The ceremony was quite private, and was held at sunrise, after the boy had sat out in the cold morning air to get chilled, so that the pain was lessened.

We have seen that each man belonged to a clan, with a clan name and a distinctive cattle-brand. Now he approached manhood, and the time when he would belong to an age-set. An age-set contains people all of roughly the same age, from different families, whereas a clan contains all the members of the family of all ages. The name for this new age-set was chosen, and each candidate had his head shaved, and received a new dress of rams' skins.

11

There were certain rules these youths must obey, and because they found these restrictions annoying, they longed for the day when they should become junior warriors (in English we call them moran; the Maasai word is *ilmurran*). Some of these rules were that they must not drink blood or touch meat, they must stay away from the enclosure until the cattle were driven in each evening, and they were not permitted to fight. Directly after initiation, if they walked around in the daytime they wore a headdress of birds' feathers. They obtained these feathers themselves, by shooting at small birds.

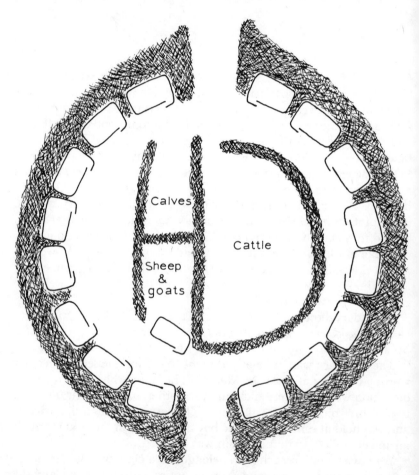

Fig. 6 This is how the houses are arranged in an *enkang*. The entrances can be filled with brushwood in times of war.

4　Young Warriors

When at last they became 'warriors', they were very proud. All the circumcised boys of a given area went together to a new enclosure called a 'manyatta'. Their houses in the manyatta were built for them by their mothers and elder sisters. These enclosures did not have a thorn fence round them, for the young men felt they could protect themselves without it. In well populated areas there might be fifty or even a hundred houses, all grouped together. The moran took his mother to live with him, and his sisters or half-sisters might accompany him, to look after him and be companions to all the other young men. Except for the mothers, it was a young people's enclosure, and they had a good time there.

The life of a moran in the old days was an exciting one. Each moran tried to kill at least one lion, and when he had done so he was allowed to wear the lion's mane on his head. Young boys picked up ostrich feathers, which they gave to their older brothers, and these feathers were made into another kind of headdress. The moran prepared himself for defending his home and the *enkang* of his family, and for attacking other homesteads, particularly those of cattle-keeping Bantu neighbours.

A young man was constantly learning new ways of behaviour. He must now stand aside if he met an elder on the path, and if an elder entered his house he must give him a stool to sit on, and go out himself. But he expected a woman to bring *him* a stool, and to place it near the door. He showed great respect to older women, and to his father's wives. He showed courtesy at all times, and particularly to his mother. He served the community by cutting poles for new houses, making cattle-bomas and building thorn fences.

Fig. 7 A moran's lion-skin headdress. (Photo: Cynthia Salvadori)

As soon as a young man went to live in the manyatta, his father gave him a spear and a shield and a sword, for his defence against attack by men or animals. He learnt about the heroes and battles of old, and how even if his side lost a fight, they must be able to say that they had not dishonoured themselves, but had killed many of the enemy. They learnt that if anyone approached holding a bunch of grass it was a sign of peace, and under no circumstances must such a person be attacked.

At all times a moran was wary in the bush. If he went to drink at a stream, he turned to face the way he had come. He could see that another moran had passed the same way by the signs he left—a knot of grass on the path, or spear marks on a tree.

Rules of eating were now different from when he was a child. A moran had to avoid eating or preparing meat in the presence of women, so a group of them went off into the bush, where they built a shelter called *ol-pul*. Sometimes the shelter was a cave or rock overhang, enclosed on the other three sides by a thorn fence.

14

Fig. 8   Moran dancing (Photo: Cynthia Salvadori)

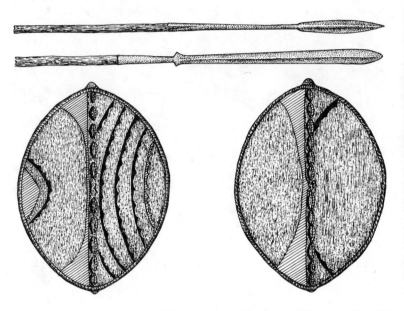

Fig. 9 Maasai spears and shields. Shield-patterns differ for the different sections. The left shield has a mark of bravery (the pattern on the left side).

A moran was not allowed to eat meat by himself, but must always be accompanied by other moran. So he learnt to consider other people and to co-operate with fellow-moran, whom he regarded as his brothers. The diet of a moran consisted of meat, the blood of his cattle, and milk. The blood he took from the neck vein of a cow by piercing it with a small sharp arrow, and caught the blood in a gourd. Sometimes he mixed the blood with milk, at other times he drank it by itself. (Nowadays a moran may also eat sweet potatoes, sugar-cane, bananas and so on, but in the past he never did.)

When the rains failed and food was scarce, the Maasai moran became particularly inclined to go on a raid. They dressed in their war headdress (see p. 14), covered themselves with red ochre, and went off in bands to raid a neighbour's cattle, or 'blood their spears' by fighting another tribe. They did not capture slaves: they killed the men, and very occasionally took the women and children home with them. The captured women were married to elders (moran were not allowed to marry), and the children were adopted and brought up as Maasai. The Maasai liked to adopt children, as they could help to herd the cows and look after the homestead.

The Laibon

The raids were organized by the leader of the age-set, *Olaiguanani*, who planned the attack, and afterwards arranged for the distribution

16

Fig. 10   Moran ready for a raiding party.

of the captured cattle, women and children. Above him was the laibon (*oloiboni*), a traditional hereditary leader, much skilled in magical practices, who controlled the behaviour and tactics of the moran, and indeed of the whole Maasai group. The first laibon, it is said, was found on the Ngong Hills, and each laibon since then has been descended from him. A laibon had to be consulted before a raid, so that he could give his consent to it. He was the person who could ask God

17

for rain. He cured illnesses and made charms and protective medicine for warriors. In fact he was consulted about all the ceremonies and decisions of the people. After a raid he was given some of the cattle, and then *Olaiguanani* divided the rest between those moran who had been particularly brave and daring, and if any were left, between the other warriors.

The moran were proud of their bravery, and wanted especially to please the laibon, and be a credit to their families. If two tribes or two Maasai sections fought each other, peace was later established by young mothers from the two sides suckling each other's babies, and the moran held grass as a sign of peace.

Young Girls

While the young men were practising the arts of war, the young girls lived with them in the manyatta as their lovers. They prepared their food for them, and were even allowed to accompany them to the *ol-pul* for a meat feast (to which older women might not go). Now at last they felt more grown-up and responsible. They ornamented themselves with coiled wire and beads, and aimed to please the young men. Later, when they were married, they would have a less idle life, but at this time they did very little real work.

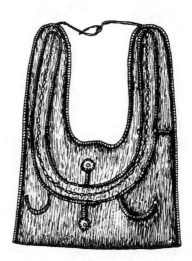

Fig. 11   A bag in which a woman may keep her necklaces and bracelets when she is not wearing them.

5   Elders

When he had been a moran for a number of years, the time came for a young man to enter into the next stage of his life. The moran left the manyatta to become elders and to marry. This could only be done with the consent of the elders, and in agreement with the laibon. The whole age-set left at the same time, and the elders prepared for this event by causing another group of boys to be circumcised. So everybody moved up a stage: old moran married and built a new *enkang*, and new moran built a manyatta. The old houses were burnt, or left to fall to pieces.

The Eunoto Ceremony

When a moran became a senior member of the community, he went through a very important ceremony called *eunoto*. The elders chose a site where the ceremony would take place, and the moran and women built their new houses in a circle, facing inwards. The elders selected 49 of the moran, usually those who had distinguished themselves in some way, and from them a leader, *Olotuno*. The mothers of the selected moran built a huge round house called *o-singira*, ornamented with cattle skulls and horns. This was a very special house, and only those moran who had led blameless lives might go into it. It was used as a kind of club-house during the *eunoto* ceremonies.

On the first day of the ceremonies the moran prayed at dawn, and then set up poles topped with ostrich feathers, and hung their lion-skin headdresses from branches of trees. They danced all day, their bodies smeared with red ochre and fat. They drank a special concoction made from the bark of a tree, which caused them to become different from their normal selves. Some of them threw fits and foamed at the mouth.

On the second day the moran painted their bodies with white patterns, dressed in coloured clothes and beads, and attached bells to their thighs. They went to the new enclosure with their ostrich-feather headdresses on their heads, and their spears in their hands. The mothers of the 49 chosen ones shaved their sons' heads, while they sat quietly waiting. It was an awesome moment when a moran's hair, which he had not cut all the time he lived in the manyatta, was shaven off and his long pigtail lay on the ground.

The third day began with the slaughtering of an ox, chosen because of its special greyish colour and markings, from the hide of which were made rings for each moran to wear. In the evening, naked and painted white, they went to *o-singira*, where they were given a great welcome by all the people. Each one led his family round this special house.

Marriage

After a man had been through the *eunoto* ceremony he was allowed to marry. The girl also had to perform certain rites before she could marry, but they were quite private. When she left the manyatta she returned to her parents' *enkang*, where she went through a form of circumcision. Her father sacrificed a ram and brought honey-beer, to ensure that she would bear many children. Her head was shaved, and she wore a special chain of tiny metal discs on her head to show that she was now ready to be a bride.

Nobody was allowed to marry within their own clan, and a man was not allowed to marry a woman older than himself. Apart from this, he was free to select his own bride, though parents may have decided whom they wanted their son to marry when he was small. The son did not necessarily have to honour this betrothal, though in many cases he did so. A man showed his interest in a girl by arranging for a gift to be given to her. Then he took gifts to his chosen girl's father and asked his consent to the marriage. They arranged the amount of cattle the husband should give, which was perhaps three cows and an ox to the girl's father, and a ram to the girl's mother. When the arrangements had been settled, and the bride-price agreed, there was a feast at the girl's home, but the two young people did not attend it. The young man had to bring animals for sacrifice to the bride's parents, and when the animals were killed their fat was used for mixing with red soil to make the ochre paste that Maasai smear onto their bodies.

The girl dressed in a new skin dress, put a new ornament in her ear-lobe, and made a ceremonial departure from her parents' house to her future husband's homestead, where she had already built herself a house. They were then man and wife, and from then onwards the man called his wife by a pet name.

Now that the girl had become a married woman, she was anxious to have a child of her own. It was expected of her, and it was regarded as a disgrace if she did not become pregnant soon after marriage.

Birth

The birth took place in the woman's own hut, and she was attended by a woman belonging to her husband's family. A sheep was slaughtered, for the mother had to eat fat and meat, in order that the child might suckle well. The women of the homestead had a joyful feast, and the next day the rest of the homestead joined in. The oxen were supplied by the father of the child. On the fourth day the child was taken outside the house to be shown the sun, and was given a name, by which he was known for two or three years, until he became old enough to run about.

On the tenth day the mother went to milk the cows, taking the new baby with her on her back. All this time the father was not allowed to go into the house, for birth was women's business, and men stayed away.

When the child could walk, the women of the family got together and killed and ate a small ram. They gave the child a new name, usually the name of someone in the family, either alive or dead, which the child bore until he became a moran. (At that time he was known as Ole So-and-so, that is, son of So-and-so.) The father also changed the name by which his relatives called him, and was now known as father of So-and-so.

Perhaps later the father took a second wife, who built her house on the left of the family gate. Some men had three wives, but there was no limit to the number provided that a man could afford to keep them. They each looked after a portion of their husband's cattle when they were in the enclosure, but they did not own cattle themselves.

A young married woman was occupied in looking after her children, and assisting the older married women in running the homestead. They did all the daily work such as preparing food, gathering firewood, fetching water, milking the cows, scraping skins free from hair, sewing the skins, and seeing to the needs of their menfolk. The older men looked after the cattle and supplied the blood and meat, and cut wood for house building. They alone were allowed to smoke tobacco and drink the alcoholic honey-beer.

The elders decided court cases—though there were few of these. A thief had to pay a fine of cattle to the wronged man, and so did anyone who broke another's bones. If a man killed another of a different clan, he had to give the other clan 49 cattle. Moreover, the fellow-clansmen of the victim might revenge their clan by killing one of the murderer's clan. There was no fine for killing a blacksmith, who, as we shall see, was regarded as different from other people.

Death and Burial

When a man or woman died, the son took the body out into the bush, to the west of the homestead, and placed it on the left side, leaving it for scavengers such as hyenas. Rich old men, or laibons, were buried under a small heap or cairn of stones, and when a Maasai passed such a cairn he added a stone as a mark of respect.

The house of a dead person was abandoned, and in some parts of Maasailand the whole homestead had to be moved. When the head of the family died, his relations killed a black or white bullock and smeared the fat on their garments, and on the clothes of the dead man. His wife had to leave her house, and build another in her husband's brother's homestead. It was now his duty to look after her and her children as though she were his own wife.

The cattle of a dead man were divided among his sons, though a man could ask that a small part of his cattle went to someone else. His weapons were also given to his sons, but if he had no sons both cattle and weapons went to his other male relations. Women did not inherit property, for everything they had belonged to their husbands, or if unmarried, to their fathers. A woman's only possessions were her clothes, her bead ornaments, and her household pots and gourds, and these were given to her daughters or other female relations.

When a person died (unless he was a very respected elder) his or her name was not mentioned again in the family, and so it happened that many people no longer knew the names of their grandfathers, or great-grandfathers. If they wanted to refer to them, they talked of the ancestor who belonged to such-and-such an age-set.

Curing Diseases

The traditional medicines of the Maasai, like their food and drink and clothing, came mainly from their animals. Sheep's fat was supposed to be good for almost anything, and it was either rubbed on, eaten, or mixed with herbs. Anybody could be a herbalist, including women, and they were paid with cattle for a cure. The giver of life, *Enkai*, was also responsible for sickness, so prayers were offered to him for the recovery of a sick person. Laibons interceded with *Enkai* for the good of the whole community, and prayed for rain at special sacred trees. The laibon was the spiritual and ritual leader of the community, and as such was a very important person.

6   Clothing and Adornment

The Maasai dressed according to the age-grade they had reached, so it was always possible to tell a moran from an uncircumcised boy, or a young girl from a married woman. But everyone dressed from the same materials: the main garment in the past was always made of animal hides, but may today be a reddish-coloured blanket bought from a store. Wire ornaments and beads were common to both men and women, but they made and wore their ornaments differently.

A young boy just wore a simple cloth, hide or sheepskin garment tied on one shoulder. He wore no ornaments, and the holes in his ear-lobes were filled with wooden plugs to keep them open and to stretch them. He was barefooted. The girl's dress was similar, but later on she wore large collars of wire and beads, and coils of heavy wire round her arms, from wrist to elbow. She had large hoops of iron wire threaded through the top fleshy part of her ears, and after her circumcision ceremony, a band of small metal pieces across her forehead from ear to ear, with two loops of the same metal discs encircling her eyes. Her cloth garment was black.

A circumcised boy also wore a black covering hanging from one shoulder, and as we have seen, he used to shoot small birds and decorate his hair with their feathers. When he became a moran he was allowed to dress much more splendidly. His garment was a decorated black tunic, again tied over one shoulder, and his hair was elaborately dressed. He was allowed to paint himself with red ochre, and cover his hair with the same mixture. The moran spent much time dressing each others' hair with red ochre, and arranging it into tiny plaits in a special pattern. The back hair was made into a pigtail, and the plaits of the

Fig. 12   Women's dress and bead necklaces.

Fig. 13   Maasai girl and old man outside one of the houses in the *enkang*.

front hair were divided into three parts, knotted together, and held in place by a wire and bead band. He wore metal earrings in his ear-lobes, and beads round his neck. On his upper arm he sometimes had an arm-ring made of horn, with two points sticking upwards. Round his neck and reaching to his waist was a long strap of hide decorated with beads. When he went to war, or on a raid, he wore an ostrich-feather headdress, or, if he had killed a lion with his spear, he wore the lion's mane on his head. He had rattles tied to his legs to make a frightening noise, and perhaps a charm given to him by the laibon.

A married man was less splendidly dressed, and his head was shaved. If he was wealthy he might wear ivory arm-bands and bead ornaments, but he was now less concerned about his appearance, and spent his time attending to his cattle instead of grooming himself. His wife continued to wear the wire and bead collars and necklaces that she wore when younger, and she hung spirals of wire by huge flat leather straps from her ear-lobes. When she had just had a child, she painted white patterns on her face and shaved her hair.

Weapons

Maasai weapons were a shield, a sword and a spear. The sword was about half a metre long and was kept in a red leather scabbard, attached to the moran's belt. His spear was about two metres long, made of iron with a holding part in the middle, painted red or black. Long ago these spears had a short fat leaf-shaped blade, but modern ones have a long thin blade. They are decorated with giraffe's hair.

At this point let us say something about the smiths who made these weapons. These people lived apart from the rest of the Maasai, and were considered inferior to them. If a smith killed a Maasai, a raiding party set out and killed several smiths; if a Maasai murdered a smith, there was no compensation due to his relatives. But smiths were very necessary, because once a spear was thrown at an enemy it might be lost, and a new one would have to be made. The smiths therefore lived quite comfortably, for they demanded sheep and goats in payment for their services.

The shield was a most important item for it not only protected the moran, but by its various patterns it identified him. A person who could read the various markings knew where a given moran came from, what his age-set was called, and whether he was particularly brave, for there was a special mark for bravery. The shields were all made of giraffe or buffalo hide stretched over wooden frames, and the patterns were in red, black, grey-blue and white. The coloured paints were made by mixing powdered stone, charcoal or ox-bones with water and ox-blood.

7 Recent Maasai History

There is a Maasai legend that Olmasinta, the founder of the Maasai, had four sons. To these sons he gave a gift; the eldest one was given the great wide pastures and the herds of cattle; the second son's gift was the fertile hill-slopes and valleys, the grain and the vegetables; the third son was given the knowledge of iron-working, and became a smith; and the fourth son had charge of the wild beasts and became a hunter. This is how the Maasai explain the origin of the pastoralists (themselves), the Bantu agriculturalists who live near them, the smiths, and the hunting Dorobo.

At the height of their power the Maasai occupied an area about 800 kilometres from north to south, and about 240 kilometres from east to west. We do not know much about their history before the late eighteenth century, for no records were kept, and we only have oral traditions and travellers' tales to go on. There seems to have been a period of peace during the eighteenth and early nineteenth centuries.

Then the Maasai became divided into those who said they were the true descendants of the founder, Olmasinta, and those who were not. The former were known as Ilmaasai, and the latter as Iloikop, or Wakwavi. During the nineteenth century these two groups fought so much among themselves that their populations were becoming dangerously low. The Iloikop were said to be more warlike than the Ilmaasai, and it is they whom early travellers and traders tried to avoid. The wars between the two were very big affairs, not just cattle raids. The Ilmaasai laibon Supet, who as a young moran had witnessed many defeats at the hands of the Iloikop, later organized the army better, and gave much good advice to the moran. At this time the Ilwuasin-Kishu, a section of the Iloikop, were the chief enemies of the

27

Ilmaasai, and because of Supet's leadership they were totally defeated.

Supet died in about 1860, and was succeeded as laibon by the famous Mbatiany, after whom one of the peaks of Mt Kenya was named. Mbatiany is said to have forecast the coming of the Europeans. During his time the Ilaikipiak were the main Iloikop section, and again there were bloody battles between the two peoples. The Ilpurko section of the Ilmaasai were driven from their grazing lands near Lakes Naivasha and Nakuru, but Mbatiany persuaded them to make one great effort to regain their territory. All their hopes were centred on this battle. The senior and junior moran went into training and practised their fighting techniques until they were confident of victory. The laibon gave them charms to ward off wounds, and the women encouraged them with their faith and loyalty. Proudly the moran left their homes, and this time their hard training was rewarded—they totally defeated the Ilaikipiak. The year was about 1880.

These battles had so weakened the Maasai that several threats, rinderpest (a cattle disease) in 1880, cholera and famine in 1890, and smallpox in 1892 almost finished them. Many families gave their children to the Kikuyu, to make sure that they were properly fed. On Mbatiany's death there was a dispute about which of his sons, Olonana or Sendeu, should succeed him. In the end Olonana (whom we now call Lenana) became chief laibon, and it was he who made treaties with the new British administration. The British mistakenly thought the laibon was the paramount chief of the Maasai, and did not at first realize that he was really the spiritual leader, especially in relation to ceremonies. In his new position as spokesman for all Maasai, Lenana went to live at Ngong, near the colonial administration in Nairobi.

Meanwhile the settlers were 'opening up' the fertile highlands, and many farmers trekked north from South Africa to start a new life in this promising country. But the traditional Maasai grazing grounds ran right across the lands the settlers wanted to farm. The colonial government persuaded Lenana that the Maasai should no longer roam freely, but should occupy two reserves, one north of their new railway, and the other south of it, spreading across the border into neighbouring German East Africa (now Tanzania). This was a blow to their independence, but worse was to follow, for the settlers soon wanted part of the northern reserve as well. In 1910–11, although Lenana opposed the move, another great trek occurred, this time of Maasai driving their cattle southwards to their new reserve (the southern reserve made larger). There they have been ever since, in an area of approximately four million hectares.

8   Folk Stories from Maasailand

The stories which follow were told to an Englishman, Mr A. C. Hollis, nearly 80 years ago. He wrote them down in Maasai, and translated them literally into English. Some of the stories are very long and very detailed, so I have simplified them in the following pages. The first story explains why the Maasai believe that all the cattle in the world belong to them.

How Cattle Came to the Maasai

The elders say that God saw a Dorobo, and an elephant, and a serpent on the earth, all living together. One day the Dorobo asked the serpent, 'Why does my body itch when you breath on me?' He was so irritated that he threw his club at the serpent and killed it. When the elephant asked where the serpent was, the Dorobo said he didn't know. But the elephant guessed, and she was sad.

After some days the elephant gave birth to a child. She went away in the long muddy grass to eat, and when she came back she drank from a puddle near the house. Now the weather was very dry, and this puddle was the only water the Dorobo had for washing and drinking. He was very angry with the elephant for making it dirty, and so he shot the elephant with a bow and arrow. The baby elephant was very upset, and he went away from the Dorobo's house, because he saw that he was bad.

When the elephant's child had gone a little way into the bush he met a Maasai moran, and he led the Maasai back to the Dorobo's house, hoping he might avenge the death of his mother. That night God told the Dorobo to come to a certain place the next morning, for he had a message for him. The Maasai heard, but the Dorobo did not, for he was fast asleep. So the Maasai went to the meeting place, and there God told him to take an axe and in three days build a cattle boma and a house for himself to live in. He told him to go and find a calf in the forest, kill it and tie the meat up in the hide. Then he should make a fire and throw the bundle of meat on it. When this was done, the Maasai was told to shut himself up in his house, and not to be startled if he heard a noise like thunder.

The Maasai did as he was told, and when he had shut himself up inside the house, God let down a strip of hide from the sky, right down to the bundle of meat on the fire. For many hours cows came down the strip of hide, one by one, into the boma. The boma became so full of cattle that they began to press against the Maasai's house, and the noise filled him with fear. He opened the door and peered out to see what was happening. At that moment God cut the strip of hide, and told the Maasai that no more cattle would come to him, because he had been afraid, and come out of the house.

Ever since that day the Dorobo has had no cattle; and the Maasai people say: 'God in the olden days gave us all the cattle in the world.'

The Woman, the Children and the Fruit Tree

Once upon a time there was a woman who had no husband and no children. She went to a medicine man who asked her which she wanted most, a husband or children? She said 'children', so he told her to go to a certain tree which bore fruit, and gather the fruit into three or four cooking pots. The woman did as she was told, and took the pots home with her. Then she went out for a walk, as the medicine man had told her. On her return the house was full of children and young people. Her work had been finished for her, her cattle tended, and moran were singing and dancing outside her house. She was overjoyed, and because there were so many people now to help her, she soon grew rich.

All went well until one day the woman got angry with the children, and she scolded them, calling them 'children of the tree'. Immediately there was silence. The boys stopped tending the cattle, and the girls left the housework unfinished. They all turned back into fruit again. The woman could hardly believe her eyes. She cried and cried, but the fruit did not turn back into children. She went back to the tree. She climbed up into the branches, to try to pick some more fruit. But she saw with horror that the fruit all had eyes, and all the eyes were staring at her. She shook with fright, and was quite unable to get down from the tree without help from her neighbours.

She never went to the tree again.

The Warriors and the Monkey

One day some moran wanted to go on a raid, so they consulted the laibon, who told them that they would not be successful if they killed any monkeys on the way. The young men laughed at this—there was no point in killing monkeys, when soon they would be blooding their spears on a cattle raid. But one young man did not laugh. He was going on his very first raid, and he was a terrible coward. He didn't want the raid to succeed at all, because he was so frightened. So as they walked along in a party, he lingered behind, and when he saw a monkey on the path he killed it.

Now when the warriors reached the region of the manyatta they were going to attack, they saw a man trapping rock-rabbits. Thinking he might warn the other moran in the manyatta, one of the raiding party threw a club at him and hit him squarely on the head. But the man only brushed at his head with the back of his hand, as if a fly had settled there. Then another man threw his club, and the same thing happened. This time the victim looked up and saw the raiding party. With a terrible roar he sprang up and rushed at them. He had no weapons, but he looked so fierce that the entire raiding party ran away. As they ran they passed the coward hiding in the bushes. They guessed what had happened when they saw the dead monkey on the path, and because of this man's treachery they put him to death.

The Warriors and the Devil

Once upon a time there were two brothers, who lived in a manyatta. One day their father gave them a bullock, and they said, 'We cannot kill it here; let us go to a quiet place where there is no man, no animal, no bird, and no fly.' They searched for such a spot for five months, and finally they found it. They killed the bullock, and then the older brother said, 'Take the bullock's stomach and fetch water in it so that we can cook some meat.' The younger brother went off with the stomach, which was like a leather bag, and he drew water from the river. Suddenly he heard the river speak.

'He has drawn water from me!' it said. He was so frightened that he ran all the way back to the camp, and as he ran he spilt the water.

'You're a coward', said his brother, when he heard the young man's story. 'Give me the stomach.'

So the elder brother went to the river, and the same thing happened. But when he heard the river speak, the young man merely said, 'Yes, I did it on purpose!' and walked back to their camp.

Then he sent the younger brother to fetch firewood. As the boy pulled the branches off a tree, he heard the branches say, 'Oh, he has broken us!' and again he was so frightened that he ran back to his older brother. The brother had no fear at all. He broke off branches, and when they cried out he answered, 'Yes, I did it on purpose!'

Well, the two brothers made a big fire, and they cooked the meat and had a good feast. Then they lay down to sleep. While they were asleep the Devil came into their shelter, and put out the fire. He had an eye which shone, just like a piece of burning charcoal. During the night the elder brother woke up, and he said to his younger brother, 'Wake up! The fire has gone out—make up the fire!' So the young man yawned and stretched himself, and still half asleep he thought he saw a glowing piece of charcoal. He reached out to use it for re-lighting the fire, but of course it was really the Devil's glowing eye. The Devil was so angry that he swallowed the boy whole.

When the dawn came, the elder brother chased the Devil all over the forest. The Devil was very frightening in the daylight. He had nine heads and one very very big toe. But the elder brother was not frightened of him. He attacked him with his spear, and he managed to cut off one of the Devil's heads. The Devil ran away, howling. But next day he came back again, and when the young man saw him he chased him, and cut a second head off. This so weakened the Devil that he could no longer run away. The young man cut off the huge toe, and out of it came his brother, still alive.